TAKI

The True Story of
Terri-Lynne McClintic and Michael Rafferty

CRIMES CANADA:

True Crimes That Shocked The Nation

~ Volume 13 ~

by Kelly Banaski

TAKING TORI

The True Story of
Terri-Lynne McClintic and Michael Rafferty

CRIMES CANADA:

True Crimes That Shocked The Nation

~ *Volume 13* ~

by Kelly Banaski

www.CrimesCanada.com

ISBN-13: 978-1530855360
ISBN-10: 1530855365

Copyright and Published (2016)

VP Publications an imprint of

RJ Parker Publishing, Inc.

Published in Canada

Copyrights

This book is licensed for your personal enjoyment only. All rights reserved. No part of this publication can be reproduced or transmitted in any form or by any means without prior written authorization from Peter Vronsky or RJ Parker of VP Publications and *RJ Parker Publishing, Inc*. The unauthorized reproduction or distribution of a copyrighted work is illegal. Criminal copyright infringement, including infringement without monetary gain, is investigated by the FBI and is punishable by fines and federal imprisonment.

This is a work of nonfiction. No names have been changed, no characters invented, no events fabricated.

Kindle Unlimited

Enjoy these top rated true crime eBooks from VP Publications **FREE** as part of your Kindle Unlimited subscription. You can read it on your Kindle Fire, on a computer via Kindle Cloud Reader or on any smartphone with the free Kindle reading app.

OR

Click 'Buy' and own your copy.

View All Books by RJ Parker Publishing at the following Amazon Links:

Amazon Kindle - USA

Amazon Kindle - Canada

Amazon Kindle - UK

Amazon Kindle - Australia

View Crimes Canada Book at:

rjpp.ca/CC-CRIMES-CANADA-BOOKS

Table of Contents

Table of Contents 5

Author's Note..6

Prologue 8

Terri-Lynne McClintic..12

Michael Rafferty..34

When Evil Collides 42

Victoria Stafford..50

The Murder 56

Missing 68

Arrest and Confession..74

Trial and Sentencing..86

Life After Murder..96

Acknowledgments..97

Books in the Crimes Canada Collection................98

ABOUT THE AUTHOR 100

Connect with Kelly..102

Author's Note

All conversations in this book are paraphrased from news articles or taken directly from court transcripts and letters from Terri-Lynne McClintic.

I would like to thank my fiancé Steven Gosse and my children for standing by my side as I went through the harrowing research for this project, and my friend Andrew Dodge for his never-ending flow of ideas. Caitlin and Tiffany at Ruby Tuesday's made long days of research much easier by allowing me to take up an entire table with my writing paraphernalia and I thank them profusely. Lucky, Hannah, Arian, Einar, Gabriel, Meadow, Ero and Tristan – I love you guys with all my heart. Thanks for putting up with me.

Prologue

If you could see defiance, repentance and remorse all wrapped up in one package, it would look like a young, strong, brunette woman with soft brown eyes and a pointy chin. Her name is Terri-Lynne McClintic. Like all things dangerous, a closer look into those soft brown eyes reveals a deadly fire that lashes out, even in guilt and remorse. Hate is her only form of reference so even her most selfless acts come out bitter with a sharp edge.

Terri-Lynne McClintic was interviewed for this book. She expressed her fears that it would seem she was making excuses, trying to explain away her guilt. She does not. She made no excuses for her crimes, but there are reasons a plenty for why she is where she is. Science and research have shown us what happens when a child is abused from a young age. The things rape and childhood abuse do to a person's psyche are mind boggling. Terri-Lynne doesn't care what the reasons are or if anyone else does, either. She asks for no sympathy and accepts our sour judgments, welcomes them, even. She is the closest thing to a feral human being I have ever encountered in modern society. Even in her remorseful, softer moments, a rage boils over in her speech and handwriting. A rage at herself for being weak, for being gullible, at the shitty lot she's been handed in life. A popular phrase in psychology is "You don't know what you don't know," and there was a lot Terri-Lynne didn't know. She didn't know you can survive without abuse. She didn't know love could come without pain. She didn't know there could be a life without an addiction.

Terri-Lynne was 18 when she met 28-year-old Michael Rafferty in Woodstock, Ontario, Canada. Four months later, the pair abducted, raped and killed tiny, blonde, 8-year-old Victoria Lynn Stafford. On April 8, 2009, the first day Tori had been allowed to walk to Oliver Stevens Public School alone, only three short blocks from her home, Terri-Lynne approached the little girl as she left for the day. Her parents never saw her again. No one did, except Terri-Lynne McClintic and Michael Rafferty. She was seen on video footage and in the mind's eye of parents who recalled the pair walking by on the last day of Tori's life. But never again would her parents hold her or hear her voice. No teacher ever taught her again. She never learned another Sunday school lesson or watched another after-school cartoon.

Terri-Lynne walked young Tori a few feet and then around the corner where Rafferty was parked. She put her in the car and the threesome drove off together. After making several stops, including one for drugs, the pair took Tori into a wooded area where she was raped and eventually killed. They buried her body under some nearby rocks where it lay undiscovered for 103 days.

Terri-Lynne McClintic

Terri-Lynne McClintic was born in 1990 in Woodstock, Ontario, to a stripper/prostitute/drug addict who danced the circuit in gentlemen's clubs all over the area. Not much is known about her other than she wasn't in a place in her career where she felt confident having a baby. She gave the baby to her best friend, fellow stripper/prostitute and cohort in frequent debauchery, Carol Sandford.

Carol raised the child alone for a while, with the help of her parents, family members and neighbors. She supported herself and the baby by dancing under the name Breese., or sometimes Victoria, and with a monthly disability check. Carol had a plethora of her own problems dating back to her own horrific childhood. Mentally scarred with a history of abuse of every nature, she had already lost custody of her own two biological children before Terri-Lynne came into the picture.

Eventually, Carol hit the jackpot. In spite of her lifestyle and OxyContin addiction, she met and fell in love with a long-haul truck driver named Rob McClintic and decided to give domestic bliss a try. The pair were married and filed for legal custody of Terri-Lynne. Despite being a stripper and prostitute with a legal rap sheet, despite being found unfit to care for her own children, despite her own sister filing a complaint with the court against the adoption, and despite being a confirmed and known addict, Carol and Rob McClintic were awarded custody of Terri-Lynne.

When Terri-Lynne was very young, surrounded by family and friends, she had the influence of Carol's parents in her life. They loved her and doted on her, as grandparents do. They remember her as a sweet girl with an open smile. She had large brown eyes and loved to be outdoors. Rob was a decent father and tried to do the right thing in his new marriage and with his adopted daughter. The first few years of Terri-Lynne's life started out normal. As normal as can be, considering she was birthed by one addict and stripper and raised by another, but there was love and some stability. Life made as much sense as it could to a two-year-old little girl.

The family unit did not hold together long, however. Rob could be gone for weeks at a time and Carol was not disposed to following anyone else's rules after having been on her own for so long. Trouble in paradise set in fairly quickly and the marital bliss dissolved into a puddle of Pabst Blue Ribbon and pain pills. Soon

Carol set off with Terri-Lynne, age 3, to start a new life. Rob McClintic saw Terri-Lynne one last time after Carol took their meager possessions and left his life with their toddler. His last glimpse of the daughter he remembered was in court during child support hearings when she was about five. He never saw her again but continued to pay child support until she became an adult.

When Carol left Rob and took Terri-Lynne with her, it changed her life forever. The world turned sour for little Terri-Lynne, and it was then that she began the metamorphosis into what her surroundings demanded of her. Throughout the rest of her life, she was not treated as a human being. She was taken at will by men who knew no one cared. She had no control over what happened to her body, her circumstances or her location. Before she was 10 years old she was abused, sexually assaulted and manipulated until there was no person left inside her. No moral code, no inner compass. The only impulse she had was to survive. The only lessons she'd learned of survival was you had to fight for it.

Terri-Lynne's childhood is a blur of constant transitioning neglect and abuse with intermittent spurts of foster homes, Children's Aid and youth detention. Carol went where the money was good. Not only did she have Terri-Lynne to support but she also had a relationship with OxyContin that demanded her constant attention. From the age of five, Terri-Lynne began to be subjected to instances of molestation and rape. Carol is quoted in the Toronto Star as saying she stopped the sexual abuse of Terri-Lynne as soon as she knew it was happening but that she hadn't known until she'd asked Terri-Lynne herself in her mid-teens, long after she had started taking care of it herself when she could.

The cure for everything to Carol was to move. To leave town and go onto another strip club, in another seedy neighborhood with new drug connections she could start fresh with. The mother/daughter pair moved incessantly, according to Rob McClintic, who said he would occasionally hear about Carol and Terri-Lynne during his long hauls. Carol had family in Strathroy and Brampton. They had also lived in Guelph, Woodstock, Parry Sound, Muskoka, Cambridge, Hamilton, and North

Bay. Terri-Lynne would start a new school once or more a year only for the other kids to find out all too soon that her mother was a stripper. Her attendance record throughout her entire educational career was intermittent, at best.

According to studies and research conducted by the American Psychological Association, the correlation between residential mobility and well-being is well documented. The most telling study consisted of 7,108 American adults, ages 20 to 75, who were followed over the course of ten years. What it showed, and other studies like it have shown, is that children who move frequently perform worse in school as well as display more behavioral issues. The participants who reported moving a lot in their childhood years also reported more problems with social relationships, psychological well-being and personality disorders. More location changes almost always mean more trouble maintaining relationships and lower life satisfaction as an adult. The results were the same even when variables like age, gender and education are controlled.

Researchers delved into deeper recesses of this study by comparing various personality types such as amicability, extraversion, openness, neuroticism, and conscientiousness to gauge the effect of considerable childhood moving on each but also how each personality type dealt with frequent childhood moves. What was discovered could also be said to be what was expected. Introverts and shy people, those who found it hard to make friends in the first place, are hindered more by many moves in formative years than those who find making friends easy. People who are outgoing and more social are least affected negatively by a lot of moving early in their lives. While it is true that moving a lot as a child makes it far more difficult to make and maintain relationships as an adult, it isn't as big a problem for some as for others depending upon their latent personality traits.

Another fairly predictable part of the studies concerned the value of neuroticism in connection with rapid childhood relocation. People who are neurotic, meaning nervous, moody and high strung, and who were subjected to multiple childhood moves were less likely to experience high levels of life satisfaction and more likely to show signs of poor psychological well-being. People who didn't move as much and were not neurotic displayed more instances of life satisfaction and psychological well-being. It is thought that this occurs because of the tendency for neurotic people to react more negatively than others to stressful life situations.

Interestingly, the mortality rate was also considered in those who moved frequently as children. It was found that those who moved a lot tended to die more frequently by the second half of the research study. This information was gleaned from an environment of controlled age, race and gender. The speculation is that moving creates a lot of stress, which we know has drastic effects on the body, both physically and psychologically.

What all this meant for Terri-Lynne is hard to say. While it points to a definite link between this portion of her unhappy childhood and her adult behavior, it certainly doesn't excuse it. Had Carol McClintic stayed with Rob, or if she'd left Terri-Lynne with her parents, or any number of other possibilities that would have reduced the harm done to young Terri-Lynne, Tori might still be with us today. Having this information is no consolation or excuse but only a portent of what can and will continue to happen as more children like Terri-Lynne slip through the cracks.

Drugs, marijuana, booze and OxyContin, specifically, were readily available in the McClintic household. Terri-Lynne began to experiment at age 8 with what she found around the house. She began with marijuana, and as her drug use skyrocketed, her educational performance and school attendance plummeted.

According to information from the Virginia Commonwealth University, Professor of Psychiatry, Elinore F. McCance-Katz, M.D., Ph.D., risk of dependence and addiction increases when the first use is before the age of 16. The human brain does not fully mature and develop until approximately age 24. Until that age, the composition of the brain changes and morphs and develops. There are three structures of the brain which are maturing during adolescence: nucleus accumbens, amygdala and the prefrontal cortex. These three structures are also involved in drug and alcohol responses, which is where many of Terri-Lynne's fatal mistakes ruminated.

The nucleus accumbens is the reward and pleasure center of the brain. The neurotransmitters dopamine and serotonin are produced here. They control feelings of desire, satiation and inhibition. Drugs and alcohol increase dopamine production and the feeling of desire and pleasure while decreasing production of serotonin and the satiety and inhibition factors it produces. In the underdeveloped brain of a child, the nucleus accumbens will direct the child to choose low effort, high excitement choices. Coupled with the effects of drugs and alcohol, there is no chance for proper decision making.

The amygdala and prefrontal cortex are also affected. Perceptions are assigned affective correlations, either positive or negative, in the amygdala. It also controls emotional reactions, which is why the underage child will more often react explosively. This area of the brain isn't fully functioning yet, and adolescents experience more explosive reactions than the controlled responses of adulthood. The prefrontal cortex is responsible for forecasting consequences, controlling impulses and judgement calls. Adolescents experience poor judgements and impulsive behaviors until these areas of the brain achieve a higher level of development.

The constant relocating left Terri-Lynne without a foundation and no way of learning how to make and maintain lasting relationships. The tenuous bond she had with her mother compounded her personality maladies and, in some ways, were the cause of them. She never learned to process and react as a regular, healthy teen girl, indeed as a regular human.

Carol had spent much of Terri-Lynne's youth in dive bars and gentlemen's clubs. If mother and daughter were home together, the environment looked similar to the drug warning PSA videos they show schoolchildren. Death metal played at all hours. A band called Necro was the usual favorite. A constant flow of drug traffic and sinister characters flowed through, someone buying, someone selling. One of those buying was Tara McDonald, young Tori Stafford's mother, who was in the throes of a full-fledged OxyContin addiction of her own in addition to other problems. Tara made her drug purchases from both Carol and Terri-Lynne.

Carol's wages provided only enough to find the pair a home in the most ghetto, run-down neighborhood in each town they moved to. Their meager, worn possessions were often left behind, taking only what was necessary, so the places they lived as mother and daughter were always bare, with sparse furnishings. The only thing plentiful in the home of the two McClintic women were men and drugs.

As Terri-Lynne grew older, she grew less tolerant. She grew less tolerant of rape, abuse and hunger. She grew less tolerant of being simultaneously used and neglected and began to venture into the streets of whatever town in which she and Carol resided to meet her needs. Her outrage and hard realizations at humanity and life itself escalated each morning she opened her eyes.

As a young child, she microwaved a small family dog until it screamed in pain. When Carol returned, Terri-Lynne blamed the dog's condition on a fight with another dog. It was put down. Police reports show when she was 16, living in Guelph, she attacked Carol, leaving her partially blind in one eye. There was one other instance where she attacked Carol hardly a year later.

Adult criminal behavior and its correlation to childhood animal abuse has long been a topic of psychological interest. Formal research, beginning as far back as the 1960's, has verified a direct connection. The wide range of adult criminal behavior as well as types of animal abuse make it a complicated subject. There is also a difference in witnessing animal cruelty and participating in it. The age of the child as well as the number of instances of cruelty perpetuated are also factors. FBI criminal profilers consider animal abuse and cruelty a sign of a future serial killer when combined with other acts. Serial killers often abuse not only animals but younger and smaller children as well. According to Psychology Today, nearly all of history's most violent crime perpetrators have an early background that includes animal abuse. The Boston Strangler; Columbine school shooters, Eric Harris and Dylan Klebold; and Jeffrey Dahmer were all connected to animal abuse prior to their crimes. Here is another sign that could have alerted someone to the sickness festering inside Terri-Lynne if only someone had known. It wasn't until after she was arrested for Tori's death that she confessed that particular crime to her godmother. Even if Carol had figured out what happened to the dog, would it have been enough to stop Terri-Lynne from future crimes? Unfortunately, there isn't any way of knowing the answer to that question. It isn't likely knowing her sick, abusive proclivities would have stopped her behavior at that point, but it may have been enough to change her course. All that we can do now is point out the fact and lament how it could have helped, had we known better.

Terri-Lynne's favorite music was from a Jewish American rapper called Necro, who claims to have invented the death rap genre. His real name is Ron Raphael Braunstein and he was born and raised in the Brooklyn area of New York in the Glenwood Houses housing projects. His music is often called horrorcore or death metal. It combines a rap and hip-hop beat with ultraviolent lyrics glorifying blood, guts and gore. Death, the occult, murder, drugs, sex and all things taboo are represented in his lyrics, and his songs are considered conceptual. Topics including the Charles Manson murders and movies like Scarface, The Godfather and Carlito's Way, all featuring savage gangsters, are intertwined throughout his albums. It was Necro that she was listening to the day of and just hours before Tori was murdered.

Canadian Children's Aid began a file on Terri-Lynne around 7 years old, and many critics of Canadian child services believe they made horrendous judgement calls throughout. Too much red tape and too many cracks to fall through left her with little chance at a successful life. She was placed in two foster homes in her formative years, usually for violence in her own home that escalated with Carol's drug abuse. Terri-Lynne's formal police record began at 10 when she stole a few toys from a local hardware store.

During the year she was 11-12, she was put into a foster home after alerting officials Carol had been abusing her. Approximately a year later, Carol was arrested for public intoxication after police saw 12-year-old Terri-Lynne running from her down the middle of the street. A few months later, Carol's boyfriend at the time, highly inebriated, threatened to slit Terri-Lynne's throat during a nightly squabble. He was criminally charged in the incident.

All the while, Terri-Lynne continued to live the way she'd been taught. She'd long ago learned to suppress any and all feelings that weren't anger, the only emotion to ever get her livable results. She continued to use OxyContin, which was prescribed for back pain, along with a whole host of other illegal substances she'd used daily throughout her formative years: marijuana, cocaine, morphine, Ecstasy, OxyContin or whatever was most prevalent in the town she was living in.

Around 8th grade, when she quit school, she had a drug overdose that left her with partial memory loss. She was a full-fledged junkie in every sense of the word by her early teens and spent the biggest part of her young life doling out extreme violence or fighting to stay off the receiving end of it.

Terri-Lynne received her first inevitable criminal charge at 15 when she flew into a violent rage at Carol's boyfriend after he asked her to move out of his home, two years after he had threatened to slit her throat and beat Carol so badly he fractured her facial bones.

A year later, Terri-Lynne found herself in a youth detention center that fed her violent streak unendingly. Incident after incident was added to her violent dossier. She attacked one resident at the youth center and four months later assaulted another, unprovoked, causing serious damage to the girl's head and face. Three more assaults occurred before she was eventually released, including one where she repeatedly kicked a girl in the head after knocking her to the ground.

Back on the street again, Terri-Lynne resumed life as usual. Once Carol gave up on her career as a dancer and began living on disability payments, money became even scarcer. Carol and Terri-Lynne would often sell their prescription OxyContin. At other times, Terri-Lynne took it upon herself to make her own money to survive.

While living in Woodstock in 2007, she took to the streets to see what she could find. Woodstock is in Southwestern

Ontario, Canada. It is the Dairy Capital of Canada, but it is in the city's own description of itself that gives a sinister air to the tale. Here, in this place that bills itself as The Friendly City, would so much death, torture and rape be meted out to certainly one of the city's friendliest citizens of all. It is also where Terri-Lynne meted out other violent acts leading up to the day she abducted Tori. She came upon two men in 2007 who seemed to her to be easy targets. She donned a bandana around her face and attempted to rob them at knife point. One of the men put up a fight and she stabbed him in the back. Witnesses to the debacle called the police. When they arrived, guns brandished, she attacked them as well, hitting one in the head, stabbing and slashing with her knife.

Her next stint in youth detention was a lengthy one. Already a tough chick, she spent her time perfecting her bad girl repertoire. While still feminine, she is extremely strong and toned, known for easily kicking off four to five hundred push-ups and 120 or more pull ups. She boxed her mattress daily and used her power and anger to bully other inmates and take their medications, food, clothing, and whatever else she wanted from them. She would often launch herself at other inmates and fight unprovoked. No one messed with Terri-Lynne. Not now. Not anymore. The lesson she had learned in the few years of her life was simple: take from them before they take from you. Only the strong survive.

She stuck to herself and didn't bring many people close. She had one friend. One girl she considered someone who at least partially understood her. That girl was released, but she and Terri-Lynne kept a correspondence for the remainder of time she was in youth detention.

The year before she bludgeoned young Tori to death, Terri-Lynne exchanged several letters with a fellow inmate, a young woman she'd met and, strangely enough, trusted. The letters were an odd mixture of graphically depicted evil deeds in girly neat script more fitting of a love letter or some heartfelt poetry.

In letter after letter, she described vile tortures and sick mutilations she fantasized about doing to anyone and everyone who she perceived had wronged her and even random strangers off the street. She described in lurid detail how she planned to attack specific inmates and staff. It wasn't long before she stopped looking for a reason to hate and began to just hate.

In one letter that was entered into evidence at trial, she wrote "I feel like a vampire in heat" and began to relate fevered, violent dreams she'd been having of slaughtering people, ripping them apart bone by bone with her bare hands. "I just want to kill someone, just see a little blood, fucking curb stomp some bitch." She wanted to go on a killing spree, she wrote, describing how she terrorized other inmates.

In another letter, she described a plan to murder another inmate's entire family upon her release and her desire to shoot a pregnant inmate in the face. In perhaps the most damaging of all the letters, she wrote about how much she would enjoy kidnapping someone, mutilating the body, smashing the skull to pieces and putting it back together like a puzzle, all the while in hopes that the victim lived long enough to experience the pain. In all the letters, Terri-Lynne referred to herself and her pen pal as "murderouz bitchez" and "real mu'fucking G's" and peppered them with Necro lyrics and the symbol of the notorious "Crips" Los Angeles-based street gang, a three-pointed crown.

Michael Rafferty

Michael Rafferty is the baby of his family. His parents already had two sons when he was born on October 26, 1980. Much like Terri-Lynne, his family moved around a lot in his early years. Unlike Terri-Lynne, however, details of his life are sketchy. He spent a portion of his youth staying with an aunt and uncle in the small village of Drayton, just outside Kitchener. He told various girls in his life he was originally from the Yukon and another that he'd lived in a farmhouse all his life. There are records indicating he attended Alexander Mackenzie in a Toronto suburb, Richmond Hill, for a short while, but little of his early life was documented.

As he told it to various women, after high school he moved to the Queen Street West area, a trendy spot for the twenty-something crowd. He studied culinary arts in the local community college. When he decided college wasn't for him, he began a string of short-term jobs. He lived in Guelph awhile and worked for a landscaping company and then a meatpacking plant. It was about this time he acquired a car. It was his most prized possession and he kept it immaculate. He visited car washes several days a week to wash and vacuum it repeatedly. His favorite thing to do was just jump in it and take off, driving anywhere and nowhere in particular. He preferred quiet back roads to more popular areas. One girlfriend, Rachael Diwell, testified in his trial that they often would simply drive around aimlessly for fun. No destination in mind.

One might find it hard to believe after glimpsing his pale, pimpled face, but Michael Rafferty made his living from the women he met. He's been described as charismatic and gentlemanly. He presented as a responsible, clean cut, friendly guy. What every girl wants. What he really was, was a skilled con-man who was at the top of his game. He had a surplus of girlfriends from which he successfully obtained money, drugs, and a place to stay. He promised each his undying loyalty. Turn-over was high, however, as each woman eventually saw the light and turned him out onto the cold, hard street, leaving him to search out new, unsuspecting prey. He bounced from job to job and continued to add to his ever growing collection of women.

In the early part of 2008, he was single, jobless, and homeless. He moved in with his mother, Deborah Murphy, and her boyfriend, David Riddall, in Woodstock. They lived on a quiet, residential street in a tidy, semi-detached home. Michael's brother, Jonathan Cundy, lived several miles away, and the two found landscaping work and contract jobs around the Toronto suburbs to keep themselves afloat. Michael began seeing a woman and moved in with her. After a predictably short romance, he moved back into his mom's place.

Living with his mom and his stepdad at age 27 suited Michael just fine. He spent his days sitting in his parked Honda Civic, playing Necro and other hard, heavy metal or racing up and down the quiet street, much to the chagrin of his mom's neighbors. Debra and David, his parents, weren't so happy with the arrangement either. His relationship with his mom was more like friendship. They gossiped about family, sent each other friendly emails and shared drug contacts. They even purchased drugs for each other. According to the neighbors interviewed by police, however, they often had huge shouting matches that spilled onto the yard and into the streets. His step-father called him a freeloader and complained that when he did manage to earn money he spent it on expensive clothes, electronics, his beloved car, and drugs.

Michael also spent a lot of time online joining dating sites, specifically those geared toward one night stands and casual sex. He described himself in his dating profiles as a romantic at heart who valued friendship above all else. He would romance his interests online and then set up a meeting. Sometimes he would date them only briefly, others he would have sex with a few times and move on. A certain few, those with money and who seemed to have completely fallen for his particular brand of manufactured charisma, he would string along for cash and his personal needs. To each one he promised a lasting relationship. He could expertly see what each woman wanted in a perfect man and he would become it, for a time. Eventually, as is the way with players and gigolos, his antics and destructive behavior became harder and harder to ignore. Only the most damaged and love starved of all the women he'd dated, Terri-Lynne, could find the time he spent with her so valuable that she would do anything he wanted to keep it.

One of the woman he was dating when he met Terri-Lynne was Charity Spritzing. She testified at Michael's trial, saying he talked her into becoming an escort and giving him the money she earned, despite having five kids at home. She claims it was at least $16,000 in six months. She and all the other women he dated were under the impression they were his one and only. They were hoping for marriage and family, and he fed that hope until a suitable replacement came along.

Michael lived with Charity for approximately two years. He used her computer regularly, and the information found on it was used in the investigation of his part in Tori's death. Searches performed and activity recorded under her account were related to veterinary schools, social media and downloaded movies. Michael Rafferty's account showed searches for underage rape, child pornography, massage parlors, epilepsy porn, urination play, necrophilia and escort services. Strangely enough, the Crown found his internet interests inadmissible in court. The jury was never privy to that information.

Michael is known to have juggled as many as seven, possibly more, women at once, using money from one to date another. Many appeared in court with lurid details of his strange sexual proclivities.

One woman signed a release form during their relationship allowing him to strangle her during sex. Another claimed in a police report he drugged and raped her although he was not charged. Some expressed uneasy feelings about his behavior around their children. Despite all their misgivings, time and again they gave him money, sex, drugs etc. Despite all of his obvious faults and his mediocre looks, he never had a problem obtaining women to do his bidding. Most often, when the general public think of murderous men like Michael, who kill with a partner, Paul Bernardo comes to mind. Paul was also a smooth talker and could easily find a date whenever he wanted, but he was also handsome in a classical sense, something Michael is not, which supplied enough of a reason for many women to look over his more obvious personality maladies.

It is unclear when or exactly how Michael Rafferty became a drug addict. In the spring of 2009 he's reported to have told an undercover police officer he had to take five 8-milligram OxyContin or 20 to 30 Percocet a day to contain his habit. In drug speak, that's how much he had to take in order to feel normal. Not to catch a buzz, or to get high, but to just not feel sick, vomit, and shake uncontrollably. If he wanted to get high, he would have to take even more than that.

Michael Rafferty somehow flew under the radar of social norms. His sick sexual fantasies and lurid habits were his own secrets. Until the death of Tori Stafford, Michael Rafferty did not have so much as a jaywalking ticket. This speaks volumes to his ability to persuade, cajole and manipulate the thoughts of those around him.

When Evil Collides

●●●●●●●●●●●●●●●●●●●●●●●●●●●●●●●●●●●●

There was something about Terri-Lynne that caused a fairly speedy end to his misogynistic behavior. Perhaps it was her obvious attraction and overly grateful reaction to even the smallest kindness he would extend her.

Michael Rafferty's drug addiction was at its highest level ever when he met Terri-Lynne. He was injecting two-to-a-line 80 milligrams pills of OxyContin each day as well as eating as many Percocet pills as he could find, usually from an old girlfriend from the meatpacking plant, Barb Armstrong. Terri-Lynne's growing loyalty and her OxyContin connections easily made her his favorite and eventually only girlfriend. "He said all the right things. It felt really good", Terri-Lynne testified during Michael's trial. One night in early 2009, they went to a movie together. After the credits rolled and the last audience member filed out, the couple had sex in the empty theater. He held her face in his hands, looking deep into her eyes, and told her he couldn't stand the thought of waking up without her and suggested they get a hotel. The love-starved teen was putty in the hands of this charismatic ne'er-do-well. It was a match made in the deepest pits of hell. He fed her need for affection, attention and love. She fed his OxyContin addiction and easily melded into any plan he had. She adored him and tried hard to please him and gain his respect despite the decade between them in age.

Michael Rafferty's constant thirst for sex was unquenchable. The unending parade of women he had relationships with attest to that. In Terri-Lynne he found a woman who enjoyed sex as much as he did, and nothing in bed was off limits to her. She could shoot as much OxyContin as he could and had better access to it. She could even earn them a modest income from sales of it. In so many ways she was his equal, yet he could still control and manipulate her. Almost from the start, they began spending and driving around in his primer black Honda Civic sedan.

The more time she spent with him, the odder things she picked up. During some of their drives he would often point out homes of single women and explain how easy it would be to break in unexpectedly and rape and kill her. Maybe it should have dawned on her sooner, like maybe the first time they had sex when he strangled her just a tad bit more than was erotic. Twelve other witnesses came forth to admit he had excessively strangled them during sex as well. It can be a consented act and a part of the sexual experience. Some of Michael's sex partners were willing but some were not.

Terri-Lynne McClintic had constructed a solid reputation for herself as a bad ass with no boundaries. It was at this time that she met Michael Rafferty. The two met at New Orleans Pizza Parlor in Woodstock, Ontario, in February of 2009. She was 18, he was 28. They began to chat as they waited for their pizzas. She says she watched him talking on his cell phone while waiting in line. He was explaining to the person on the other end of the conversation that he was lost and wasn't quite sure where he was. Terri-Lynne interrupted his conversation and explained his whereabouts. Things quickly became flirty with Michael calling her "a cute number" as he hung up his phone.

He offered her a ride home and she accepted with glee. The pizza sat chilling in the box as the two of them sat in the car in her driveway. He wrote his phone number onto the box and they talked about OxyContin, partying and found they had a lot in common. Michael suggested they go for a drive around Woodstock and Ingersoll as they talked more about drugs, movies and things they liked to do. They had sex in the car. She claimed in court records that he climbed on top of her and strangled her at one point during the act but stopped and afterward took her home. She went in with a cold pizza and a phone number for "Mike" written on the box. She didn't even know his last name.

Terri-Lynne's tough reputation would never allow her to call a guy on the next day. Not only that, but it wasn't her style to do such. She was used to men taking advantage of her. Even if she gave it consensually, sex was never enough to keep someone's interest for long. It never occurred to Terri-Lynne that a man would be interested in seeing her again. She had her hands full just existing in the tumultuous environment of her family home. Surprisingly, Michael showed up at her house a few days later to ask why she hadn't called. It tickled her to know he had been thinking of her, and the two began a strange relationship. He started to simultaneously romance and buy drugs from her, but the pair was hesitant to call each other boyfriend/girlfriend. Michael was fairly new in the Woodstock area and amazed at his new protégée's multiple contacts in the local drug scene. She seemed too young to be so well established in her debauchery, but Michael would soon learn that Carol played a big part in that scenario. Michael spent the next few weeks popping in at Terri-Lynne's house and she would sell him OxyContin. They would inject it together, smoke pot and have sex. Once they went to the movies and spent the night together in a motel.

No one had ever spent so much time and effort on Terri-Lynne, and she felt the closest thing she ever had to love. "He said all the right things," she said in court. "It felt nice." (Guelph Mercury) Although neither would admit to being in a relationship, they were rarely apart. In two short months, she would kidnap, violently torture and savagely murder an eight-year-old girl for the love of a man who she didn't claim as her own.

When Michael met Terri-Lynne, his philandering slowed considerably. He didn't have the time he once had to invest in it because he was spending more and more of it with Terri-Lynne. He had finally found a woman who hung on his every word, no matter what it was. He told her she was beautiful, that she was clever and that she was important. While all the other women in his life eventually caught on to his game and left, or ran for their lives after one of his sexual choking escapades, Terri-Lynne was more than happy to find him drugs, to ride around Woodstock doing his bidding, and to allow him to choke her during sex. In addition, she fed into every sick fantasy he ever mentioned. Even if she balked at one of his ideas, it was in such a way that it still seemed acceptable. Nothing was too weird. Nothing shocked her. She took it all in with the banality of that not unlike a shell-shocked soldier of war or child refugee of some third-world country.

In Terri-Lynne's police confession, she explained how, as their relationship progressed, he became more flagrant about his true sexual desires. It started during their many rides throughout the nearby towns. He would point out homes where he knew single women lived alone, always mentioning how easy it would be to break in and rape, torture and murder the unsuspecting woman. He even knew the exact floor plan of many of the homes he pointed out.

Later, he began to case out elementary schools and parks. They would slowly ride by an elementary school as children filed out and he would point out a specific child, always a tiny blonde girl. A child he would take, if he could. A child he would rape and murder.

"Look at her. Someone like her would be perfect. It would be so easy. We need to get one really young. The younger, the better, easier to manipulate."

At first it was like a joke, Terri-Lynne would later say in her confession. He would say things to shock her, or so she thought. Then came the day he asked her if it would be "weird" if he were to ask her about kidnapping someone. She knew he was serious after that, and in her confession she told police that she began to ignore the things he said she knew were wrong. She claims to have wanted to finally have found a man that would stay with her, so she ignored what was in front of her in the hopes that it would go away. It never did, however. It just got worse and worse. "He would say things like 'You're not going to do it are you? You're too scared aren't you?'" In the months and weeks preceding Tori's murder, Michael asked Terri-Lynne every day if she would "do it" on that day.

Victoria Stafford

Victoria Elizabeth Marie Stafford lived to be eight years old. On April 8, 2009, she dressed herself in a Hannah Montana jacket, green t-shirt and a denim skirt and topped off the outfit with a pair of butterfly earrings borrowed from her mother. Her mother also allowed a dab of blusher and a shiny swipe of lip gloss. They had just moved to a new home and Tori planned to celebrate in her new bedroom that night with a movie night and her best friends. She slipped on her black and white shoes, grabbed her Bratz purse and headed out the door to school for the last time. The first day she'd been allowed to make the short trek alone would also be her last.

Tori, as her friends and family affectionately called her, was a bubbly, precocious blonde with a vivid imagination. She lived at home with her mother Tara McDonald, her stepfather James Goris, and her older brother Daryn "Duder" Stafford. The blonde pixie's cute and contagious smile gave her a distinct Tinker Belle aura that drew smiles from even the most curmudgeonly of neighbors. She was a tiny mixture of huge characteristics. She was bold and brash, timid and shy. "She was spunky, funky..." says her mother, Tara McDonald. "One minute she'd be wearing a dress with pantyhose and tappy shoes and she was all dressed up with her hair did and everything and she'd be outside digging up worms and bugs." She was known to be a chatterbox and had been late home from school on a number of occasions because she'd stopped to talk and play with her friends. While she was precocious and energetic, she didn't seem to be the kind of kid who would be an easy snatch for pedophiles and baby snatchers.

Tori was as loved and adored as any 8-year-old girl could be, but her family was not without its problems. Tara McDonald fought her own demons with Oxy addiction and had on more than one occasion been to the McClintic home to purchase drugs. She was familiar with Terri-Lynne on a neighborhood basis as they lived only blocks away from each other. She'd also visited concerning the breeding of Tori's family Shih Tzu dog, Cosmo, with the McClintic's dog, Precious. Tori adored the dog. She spent hours playing with it and called it her bestest friend, dressing it in little outfits and rubbing its tiny paws.

Tori arrived to school on that fateful day in her usual jovial, giggly mood. Jennifer Griffin Murrell, the teacher of Tori's mixed 2nd and 3rd grade class, remembers her as full of energy and mischief that day. Tori had come to her after recess asking to go home to change her tights, explaining she'd fallen in a mud puddle. After some teacherly investigating, Ms. Murrell discovered it wasn't so much a fall as it was a happy jump into the puddle of mud. She used the incident as a teaching tool and explained that the tights would dry after only a little bit of discomfort.

They sang O Canada, practiced language lessons, had a bit of math instruction and then spent part of the day learning to research plants on the computer. During art class, Tori entertained the class by pretending to cut the decals from her t-shirt which landed her a few minutes of time out in her seat. In court, Murrell described Tori as a mother hen type to her fellow classmates. The last time she laid eyes on her was just as the 3:25 bell rang. She had forgotten those butterfly earrings her mother had loaned her and had raced back to class to retrieve them. She waved goodbye to her teacher and walked down the sidewalk to her death.

Laura Perry was picking up her son Jacob, Tori's classmate, when she saw little Tori Stafford walk by chatting with a young woman in a big, fluffy, white coat. She'd begun to allow her own kids a little freedom and had recently begun walking only partway to drop off and pick up Jacob and his older brother Zachary. She stood several meters from the school atop a small hill and waited for her boys, noticing Tori and the woman with her and their quick, purposeful gait. Laura testified in trial that she sensed something was off. She knew she'd never seen Tori with the woman and hadn't seen the woman at the school before. Her eyes welled up and her voice wavered slightly with the what-if thoughts that go through witnesses' minds after a horrible crime takes place. The time stamp on a nearby surveillance camera read 3:32.

The Murder

The morning Terri-Lynne McClintic murdered Tori Stafford began like every other in her wretched, drug-addled life. There was no food in the house, so after smoking some marijuana, she went to a local church and obtained a voucher for groceries. After going on to an employment center and filling out paperwork to help her find a job, she submitted a resume that listed her work experience as babysitting children from 8 months old to five years as well as previous positions held with Tim Horton's, as well as an industrial cleaner and as a kitchen assistant. She had a lapse in work beginning in November of 2008 which she blamed on her 8th grade education. As her strengths, she listed herself as being an outgoing, energetic, and a quick learner; she admitted she angered easily but mentioned she was always able to maintain control. She went grocery shopping with her voucher at that point and returned home to shoot herself up with OxyContin.

That's when Michael Rafferty knocked on her door and the two loaded up in his car and headed out for their usual road trip around the neighborhood hot spots and drug houses. Except this time, they ventured into something far more despicable than they had ever gone before.

Terri-Lynne had learned that ignoring Michael's strange sexual rantings or playing along as if it were just another oddball thing he'd come up with was the fastest way for it to pass. Conversations had thus far been limited to his deep desire to rape and torture a little girl and her encouragement, even though it wasn't always wholehearted. She claimed in court never to have truly believed him. She always dismissed it as so much bravado and a sick, drug-addled mind looking for ways to sound tough and mean. She may have even believed it was his way of impressing her with his outlaw ways. She only knew that he had so far been the best man she'd ever been involved with and she wanted to keep it that way.

On that fateful day, however, as they drove past Oliver Steven Public School as per usual, Michael Rafferty slowed to a crawl and asked Terri-Lynne if she was "going to do it today". According to trial transcripts, she answered, "Do what?" Although she knew what he was referring to because of all their previous conversations of his sick fantasies, she feigned ignorance. "I knew it!" Terri-Lynne claims he responded. "I knew you were all talk and no action." Those words were a trigger for her. Something in her malformed brain does not allow her to feel slighted or insulted. She would prove her own perceived merit, even if it meant taking a life.

She got out of the car and approached the first girl she saw, Tori Stafford. Michael had parked his Honda Civic just around the corner and sat waiting. He'd given her instructions during their many conversations on his fantasies and, although it was always hypothetical, it was enough to help her successfully kidnap an eight-year-old girl from her school in small town Woodstock, Ontario, Canada.

Terri-Lynne, covered in a billowy, white coat, her dark hair dragged back in a halfhearted ponytail, bent down to Tori's eye level. It was after 3 o'clock on 04/08/09. "Do you know what a Shih Tzu is?" she questioned with a friendly smile. Tori nodded and returned the smile. She *did* know what a Shih Tzu was because she had one herself. "Well, have you seen one around here because my little girl's has run off." Terri-Lynne finished with a cursory searching glance complete with furrowed brow and pursed lips.

There isn't much more pressing to an 8-year-old girl than a lost little puppy. Tori cast her own furtive glances around her searching for puppy signs. "I can show you just what she looks like. I have two of her pups in the car. They will be hungry and sad if I don't find her. Would you like to see them?" Of course she did. Terri-Lynne walked her to the Honda. As the two females approached the car, Michael became agitated and excited, yelling 'Hurry up!" Within seconds Tori was crumpled in a tiny heap on the back floorboard under Michael's coat.

Michael could barely contain his excitement. He had waited what seemed like a lifetime for the darkest and deepest of his sexual fantasies to come to fruition, and now that it had, he intended to take full advantage of the situation. The Honda Civic and its three occupants first headed out of Woodstock toward a Guelph dealer and purchased a few Percocet pain pills. The bright, quick-witted young girl knew she was in trouble from the moment she landed in the car. She pleaded to be released, promising never to tell anyone what happened. "I'll just tell my mom I stopped at my cousins' to play," said the sweet, tiny blonde as she bargained for her 8-year-old life. Michael barked orders for her to lie down on the floorboard and shut up. He turned to Terri-Lynne. "She's too damn old!" he yelled at her. "I told you it should be someone really young." "She was the first one I saw who was alone," Terri-Lynne explained.

During the two-hour drive to Guelph, it became obvious Michael was not completely happy with his girlfriend's choice of victims, but it was too late to turn back. He removed the battery from his cell phone and pulled out the dance music CD to tune in local radio stations, listening for missing children's reports. Tori was terrified. Terri-Lynne tried to keep her quiet by comforting her. She asked her questions and talked with her. Tori told her she loved Disney programs Hannah Montana and The Suite Life of Zack and Cody. She loved Christmas and Halloween best of all holidays, her favorite color was purple. The more she talked, the angrier he became. "Turn the fuck around and quit talking to her," Michael snapped.

Terri-Lynne continued to talk with her, to reassure her, soothe her into her violent death. "When can I go home?" "Soon. I won't let anything happen to you," Terri-Lynne lied. Had there been any truth to that statement, she would have released the girl or found help during one of the three times she wasn't in Michael's presence. When they arrived in Guelph, Michael drove to the dealer's home and left the two girls in the car. He left them alone in the car again when he stopped at a Tim Horton's donut store to get drinks.

Terri-Lynne didn't ask for help. She didn't set Tori free. She sat there in the car with her and lied to her. "Keep quiet," she'd say. "It won't be much longer. I will keep you safe." Whether or not Tori believed Terri-Lynne, she had no choice but to do as she was told and await the unknown. They left the drug dealer's house with a small baggie of prescription pain pills in search of an ATM and a Home Depot store. Michael pulled into the parking lot which also had a gas station with an ATM attached.

Terri-Lynne on security camera at a Home Depot buying a hammer (used to kill Tori) and garbage bags. April 8, 2009

He jumped out to use it, leaving Tori and Terri-Lynne in the car alone again. Once he'd retrieved the cash, he gave it to Terri-Lynne and dropped her off at the doors to Home Depot. Security cameras had captured images of Tori and Terri-Lynne outside the school, Michael at the

ATM and of Terri-Lynne on this macabre shopping trip. She is plainly seen wandering the aisles and perusing the shelves. She looks like any young woman embarking on a do-it-yourself journey. Only in hindsight does her choice of a claw hammer and heavy duty trash bags seem grotesque and evil.

The death march then began in earnest. They drove to an abandoned field and county road near Mount Forest. There were sparse trees and bushes but enough to shield them should anyone pass by. Michael and Terri-Lynne got out of the car. Michael walked around the car to Terri-Lynne's side. "What now?" Terri-Lynne asked, although she already knew. "Well, obviously I'm going to fuck her," he replied "We can't keep her and we can't take her back." He opened the back door of the Honda and slid in next to Tori. The next few hours were a violent blur of pedophilic rape and sadistic torture. Terri-Lynne wandered around the field surrounding the car.

"Creepy crawling, in ya crib, we're comin' to kill. Catch you while ya sleep, wake up to a gun in ya grill. Doing Satan's business, tie you up, hang you 22 cal. Bang you – Mephisto with a pistol." Necro blasted into her ear from her Ipod. She walked wide circles around the car, concentrating on the music, the lyrics. Anything and everything that wasn't what was going on in that car, a scene she had all too often played in herself. He told her to take Tori into the bushes to urinate. She held the little girl's hand and led her behind the bushes. She watched her pee and saw the blood running down her legs as they trembled. "I'm sorry. You're strong," she told Tori, and meant it. "As strong as you are?" "Oh, no. Much stronger than me." She walked her back to the car as the little girl began to cry. Despite the blasting in her ears, she heard the car door open and Michael call her name from three meters away. "Please don't go, T. Don't leave me," she held onto Terri-Lynne's hand with all her strength. She was still screaming as Michael dragged her back into the car. Again Terri-Lynne waited nearby as her boyfriend defiled and destroyed tiny Tori.

Tori's piercing screams and howls of pain melted seamlessly into the bloody, violent lyrics. Terri-Lynne knew in her heart from the very beginning that there was no saving Tori. Just as there had been no saving her. To her, preying upon the weak is a necessity and something she experienced every day. Still, it angered her in some arcane way and anger was good. Anger means protection. Anger gets shit done. The door to the back seat opened and Tori was tossed onto the snowy ground in only a T-shirt. Michael crawled out after her. His pants were around his thighs. He began to pour bottled water over his hands and genitals. Once dressed, he returned his attention to Tori lying crumpled, bleeding and crying in the snow. Viciously kicking and stomping her, he stopped, breathing heavily, and looked over at Terri-Lynne. She says that she doesn't know why she did what happened next. She has no clear memory of it. It's vague and dream-like but she knows her head filled with rage as she watched Tori writhing half naked in the frozen fields. She re-lived her own rapes and relived her own abuse. Tori's screams crossed with Terri-Lynne's rage had ignited.

She stomped heavily and quickly over the three meters of frozen land and grabbed the claw hammer and garbage bag and began raining blows down upon her. The claw hammer ripped and tore not only Tori's small frame but the very fabric of Woodstock, Ontario, Canada. When the small blonde stopped screaming, stopped moving, Terri-Lynne stopped swinging. She stumbled back a few steps and wiped her hair away. Slowly, she walked back to the car and retrieved the garbage bags. Her clothes, backpack, and empty water bottles, the hammer, Terri-Lynne's white coat and Michael's bloody shirt all went into another bag. Michael was on top of the world. His sick, longtime fascination finally realized, he was beside himself. He carried Tori's body a few meters away to a shallow dip in the field covered in a pile of rocks. The pair dug out a small spot and stuck Tori's body inside the garbage bag under the rock pile where she lay undiscovered for the next four months. They placed the final stone and took a few steps back to survey the scene. Michael turned Terri-Lynne to face him. "You're in it just as far as I am. There's no turning back now." Back in the Honda, they headed to a car wash in Cambridge, Ontario, where they tossed the bag containing the murder weapon, Tori's backpack and their bloody clothes in a dumpster. They washed and vacuumed the car. Terri-Lynne used a pocket knife to cut blood stains out of the upholstery. They changed clothes, throwing their shoes onto Highway 401 on the way back to Woodstock. They were quiet on the ride home. Terri-Lynne was still high from her day's drug consumption -- marijuana and a syringe full of Oxy earlier and the Percocet they'd shared before the rape and murder of Tori. They argued at the onset to never again speak about what they had done. They went back to Woodstock and resumed their lives. Michael replaced his battery and made a few calls.

Missing

MISSING CHILD

If you have any information about VICTORIA STAFFORD
please contact the Woodstock Police Department:
(519) 537-2323 or call 911

LOCAL MISSING CHILD FROM WOODSTOCK
LAST Seen AT OLIVER STEPHANS PUBLIC SCHOOL

VICTORIA STAFFORD
Last seen Wed. April 08 2009 3:30 p.m.

Both Terri-Lynne and Michael slipped unnoticed back into the fabric of their lives. Back to their parents' homes. Back to their addictions, job searches and everyday hustle. They had become monsters, but no one could tell. Their evil deed was not apparent. It didn't change their countenance or behavior. It did, however, change them mentally. They continued to see each other almost daily. Michael always wore his black pea coat now. The one he used to keep Tori covered in his back seat. Terri-Lynne helped her neighbors hand out flyers about the little girl who went missing, Tori Stafford.

Tara McDonald woke up that April morning and went about her regular daily activities like every other morning. Her family had recently moved into a new house, and she had a full day of organizing and cleaning ahead of her when she woke her daughter, Tori, for school that morning.

Tori's mind was also on the family's new location. To celebrate the move and to christen her new bedroom, she'd planned to host a movie night that evening complete with popcorn, sodas and snacks. She'd laid her school clothes out the night before, and the slight blonde dressed and readied with a palpable excitement in anticipation of the day, none of the usual grumbles. She wore some of her favorite items that day as well as her mom's butterfly earrings and her sweet smelling lip gloss and embarked on the last day of her life. Tara spent her day in her normal fashion, taking care of her home and family, running errands, paying bills, shopping. She also spent time doing normal family life things while battling addiction. Addiction may seem an out-of-the-ordinary issue but it is, in fact, quite ordinary.

The town of Woodstock is well-known by authorities as a problem area for the drug OxyContin. It was repeatedly shown on the national news and in newspapers. Tara had developed a dependency on pain pills. She was aware of it and actively battling it with visits to an addiction management clinic and support venues.

Terror did not immediately set in when Tori was late getting home from school. There was always someone to talk with or something to look at for the sunny 8-year-old. She was notorious for stopping off at the homes of friends and relatives on her way home from school, barely giving herself time for homework or chores. It was something along the lines that Tara expected as the minutes ticked by without

Tori. After an hour had passed, Tara began to walk the neighborhood. She walked the three blocks to Tori's school, growing more and more uneasy as time passed and no one had seen her. Family and neighbors joined in the search until nearly 6 p.m. when it became clear she hadn't just wandered off to play. Tori's grandmother called the police and she was officially a missing person.

The search for Tori began in the standard way of searching her home and the one she'd just moved from. Moving children assumed missing are found sleeping tucked away somewhere in the family home. Woodstock police Detective-Constable Sean Kelly was a major player throughout the abduction/homicide investigation. The colloquial town was turned upside down in the days following Tori's disappearance.

A tiny innocent girl snatched in broad daylight seemed implausible in their safe, quiet midst. People searched for an answer that made sense, and many decided that Tara McDonald almost certainly had something to do with it. Somehow it made more sense that Tori's own mother would harm her as opposed to someone else in Woodstock. Detective-Constable Kelly conducted lengthy interviews with friends, family, and neighbors after searching the family home, and thus began the extensive search for Tori. The first week the police worked 15 to 20 hours. They were overwhelmed. Detective-Constable Kelly kept in close contact with Tara and her boyfriend, James, as well as Tori's father, Rodney Stafford. Tara and Rodney had separated some time earlier and Rodney hadn't seen his daughter in several months.

A few days into the investigation, a surveillance video of Tori leaving her school yard with a dark-haired woman in a white coat was released. A friend of Tara's saw the images and told her she thought the woman was Terri-Lynne McClintic. When Tara took a look for herself, she also thought the woman bore a striking resemblance to Terri-Lynne, the girl she'd just bought pills from. So it was four days after Tori's disappearance that Tara McDonald called Detective-Constable Kelly with her belief that it was Terri-Lynne in the video. It was found Terri-Lynne was wanted on a violation of probation and she was arrested on April 12, 2009.

Arrest and Confession

While being held at Genest, a London, Ontario, youth detention center, she and Michael remained in as close contact as they ever had. They spoke on the phone whenever possible. He visited often and they exchanged letters at a rate of more than two or three a week at times. There was no doubt for either of them this could easily be the end of the road for them both. With Terri-Lynne behind bars, she understood Michael's concern and repeatedly consoled him, saying she would take all the blame if they were somehow found out.

She later told a jury in Michael Rafferty's murder trial that, over and over, she reassured him she would take the blame. He would repeatedly ask her if she was absolutely sure she knew what that entailed. Her answer was always a resounding "Yes." She felt his life was more important than hers. She told him more than once that she was just an 18-year-old junkie and he could still make something of his life.

Sometimes they talked about planning her escape, wondering if there was any successful way to make it happen, and shared dreams of living lives on the run like a modern Bonnie and Clyde. Together forever. They also made plans in case she was questioned in the case. They'd both seen the news reports of Tori's disappearance. Her white coat had become famous. On an afternoon visit, Michael instructed Terri-Lynne to say she and Michael had been miles away window shopping and spending a leisurely afternoon in Oakville, Ontario, visiting a Fred Astaire dance studio as Michael felt he had natural dance skill and planned to enhance it.

A second scenario was to admit being the woman in the white coat with Tori on the surveillance video, but that she'd only walked with her a short way after recognizing her as Tori McDonald, the dog breeder's daughter, although by all accounts they had never met. In yet a third concocted alibi, they discussed saying they had indeed picked her up but had dropped her off again in a green sedan. When planning Tori's abduction, they had agreed to never speak of it again once it had occurred, but that seemed to be all Michael wanted to talk about after Terri-Lynne was incarcerated. He'd even asked her to make sure she was jailed somewhere she could get conjugal visits.

During their last visit on May 12, 2009, sitting in the common room at Genest, planning what to do if the shit hit the fan, Michael grabbed Terri-Lynne's face in both hands and kissed her quickly. With a soft chuckle and a shake of his head, he told her, "You'd do anything for a little bit of love, wouldn't you?"

Tori's mother, Tara, had become positive that Terri-Lynne was the woman they were looking for, the woman who, at the very least, had last seen her daughter. Repeatedly she called authorities with her suspicions beginning April 12th, four days after Tori disappeared. Days ticked by like months as the search for Tori continued. With no clues other than the grainy surveillance video, neighbors, townspeople, and the public at large began to look toward Tara with a more skeptical eye.

Facts of her drug use and methadone clinic visits traveled through the neighborhood. Slowly, Tara McDonald became a suspect in her own daughter's murder.

News crews were camped at the family home at all hours. Tara would come out once a day to update the press, and she was often smiling and laughing. She jovially called them her "one o'clocks". The grieving process of parents is always under a social microscope. What is and isn't appropriate behavior for a grieving parent is judged and measured by those with no experience in such atrocities. No one knows what it feels like to have a child missing until it happens to them. Dealing with grief is a very personal experience that exhibits itself in varied and personal ways. Tara's soft smiles and congenial attitude was determined suspect by those in attendance at each press conference. Even the fact that she willingly gave the public updates appeared questionable, despite the fact that the reason Tara did it was only to shine more light and draw more focus to her missing daughter. There were some strange incidences that also aided the public scrutiny of her. She told the press about a mysterious late-night limo ride with a man who claimed to have information about Tori and the psychic mediums she'd been in contact with to find her daughter.

Suspicion of Tara, Tori's father and step-father certainly played a role in why they were asked to take polygraph tests. Tara failed two of the questions on the test and then raged out of the police station when accused of withholding information. Police also installed hidden surveillance devices and wire taps in the McDonald home. Tara was seen crushing and snorting OxyContin before one of her "one o'clocks" during which she denied drug use and connections that may have had a bearing on her daughter's case. Tori's father, Rodney Stafford, also became distrustful of Tara. He began attending the daily news conferences, arriving a few minutes early to wait inside, always carrying a small hidden tape recorder.

While Tara was indeed a strange bird, she did not appear to be behind her daughter's disappearance. She had told police only four days after Tori's disappearance who the woman in the video was, and so did others. Terri-Lynne's neighbors had seen that footage, too, and also saw the resemblance. She gained even more skeptical suspicion after cutting her long, dark hair that was so visible in the videos, telling neighbors she had gotten bubblegum in it. Some neighbors went to police with their theories, and others even began to surreptitiously video the comings and goings at the McClintic home.

By early May 2009, America's Most Wanted TV show featured the case, a police sketch of a woman thought to be involved was circulated, and the Ontario Provincial Police had taken over the case. The daily press conference also got a little murkier. On May 8, 2009, Tara passionately implored spectators to stop focusing on her as a suspect and concentrate on finding Tori. Four days later, she stated her belief that Tori was still alive and read an open letter to her, encouraging her to stay strong. Another three days later, Tara and Rodney Stafford, Tori's father, verbally sparred for the press with Rodney chastising Tara's lack of emotion and Tara chiding his tears as simple guilt from an absentee father. Tara, like every mother in her shoes, was desperate to find her daughter. In another attempt to bring the focus back to Tori, she laid bare all her shortcomings, the 2 to 3 uses per week of OxyContin, her two years visiting methadone clinics to clean up, and her seemingly unconcerned demeanor when Tori disappeared.

While Victoria Day walks were organized and carried out and police arranged for various local women to come in and walk for them to compare gaits with the woman in the video, Tori's killer sat in jail on a probation violation with no clue that she was becoming a more likely suspect with each passing day. Tara McDonald was a drug user, a mother who didn't walk her 3rd grader home or call police until hours after her disappearance, but she was also taller and heavier than the white-coated woman on the surveillance video, and her gait in no way matched the mystery woman's. Tara and Terri-Lynne's neighbors had more than once pointed the finger at Terri-Lynne, and so police pulled her from her cell for a short walk to observe her gait. It was so close to the mystery woman; they took her aside for questioning.

The following day they pulled her in again, and that was the day the dam broke. She began to spill the beans in a confession that would last hour upon hour. She detailed the weeks before the murders, telling of Michael's constant urging to kidnap a young girl, and finally the day they did it. The quietly horrid details of how easily "street-proofed" Tori had been led away to her death emerged.

The first few hours of her interrogation tapes show her relating the vile story with tears, choking out some of the words as if they stuck in her throat. When investigators left the room, however, she would quietly go back to her coffee and gaze around the room, only to wipe away dry tears when they returned. She did not keep her promise to Michael. Instead of taking all the blame, she took only a portion and revealed his part in the scheme.

Michael Rafferty was brought in for questioning on May 20th and subsequently arrested. He sat for six hours shivering and crying. He denied ever having a single thing to do with Tori or her disappearance. He seemed unbreakable. Repeatedly, the investigators would tell him Terri-Lynne had confessed, that they had DNA evidence in his car and belongings, but he never cracked.

Terri-Lynne, with some difficulty after the frigid spring weather, helped police find Tori's body.

Tori's body was found under a pile of rocks

The body was identified as Victoria Stafford on July 21, 2009. She explained the Home Depot surveillance footage and the timeline of events, describing the torture, rape and murder of tiny Tori in a matter-of-fact way that both chilled and confused authorities. Law enforcement arrested Michael Rafferty and Terri-Lynne McClintic for the murder of Victoria Stafford. Rafferty was charged with first-degree murder and kidnapping. McClintic was charged with kidnapping and being accessory to murder after the fact.

Terri-Lynne taken into custody on May 20, 2009

Rafferty arrested for murder of Tori Stafford

Trial and Sentencing

Terri-Lynne McClintic's trial was about as cut and dry as they get. She admitted to her part in the death of Tori and disputed no real facts. She apologized to the family of Tori and, on April 30, 2010, was sentenced to life in prison with a parole chance after 25 years. Authorities placed her plea under a stringent publication ban that was not lifted until December when the Supreme Court refused to hear a plea for extension.

Rafferty's trial went a bit differently than McClintic's. Before it even began, Crown and defense lawyers agreed to a change of venue outside of Tori's hometown to ensure a fair trial. It was decided the trial would be held in London, Ontario. Under a strict publication ban, Michael Rafferty's pre-trial motions began. Security issues were so prevailing; it was determined Rafferty would spend the whole of the trial inside the prisoner's dock. Other pretrial motions decided were that the jury would be required to visit the scene of Tori's death and where her remains were found. Specific media rules were also set forth concerning the amount and type of trial coverage. Jury selection began on February 27, 2012. Screening for the 12-person jury took approximately a week, and more than 1,000 people participated. Once chosen, they were told to expect the trial to last at least three months.

The trial itself began on March 5, 2012, with Rafferty pleading not guilty to all charges. Lead prosecutor Kevin Gowdey used his opening statement to warn the jury that they would hear and see some of the most horrific things they ever would encounter in their lives. He described the manner of Tori's death and the exact injuries she suffered. In graphic detail, he described the hammer blows to her tiny head, the body kicks and broken ribs, and, finally, the rape. Gowdey wrapped it up by promising to show the jury irrefutable evidence that Rafferty was a child-raping murderer.

Emotions ran high from the first moment of the trial and stayed at the absurdly high keel throughout. One of the most poignant moments was Tori's teacher's testimony. She cried heavily throughout it, describing the always happy, bubbly little girl and their interactions on the day she died. She spoke of the butterfly earrings Tori was so proud to have borrowed from her mother.

The next day, March 7, was even more harrowing. Tara McDonald, Tori's long-suffering mother, took the stand. She testified to her previous relationship, however fleeting, with Terri-Lynne McClintic and her mother Carol. She told the court she had seen her on two occasions, neither of which time was Tori present. She and her boyfriend, James Goris, had shown up at the mother/daughter dwelling, which she described as dirty and dilapidated, to purchase OxyContin. They had spoken of breeding their dogs together, but it never came to fruition. The meetings, as best she could recall, took place in January or February of 2009.

As heart-wrenching and soulfully torturous as those two testimonies were, the jury was still unprepared for the testimony of Terri-Lynne McClintic, who had had plenty of time to sit in her cell and continuously replay what she and Michael had done since her trial. She thought not only of what they had done to Tori, but what he had done to her and what he was capable of doing to others if she kept her promise to him and took all the blame for the killing. During her lengthy confession, both video and written, she told the lurid tale of kidnapping, rape, torture and murder, but to hear it in her own voice, spoken aloud in front of Tori's family, neighbors and peers, was practically intolerable.

Terri-Lynne first took the stand against Rafferty on March 13. Her voice cracking, low and wavering, she related how Tori's death took place. From the first time she met Michael and the discovery of his sick secret desires to the very instant Tori took her last breath and then beyond, she told the tale. She also revealed why she didn't stick to her promise to take the fall; she had thought too long and hard about what he would do if he somehow was cleared of Tori's murder because of her. He would kill again. He would find another, younger little girl and perform the same hideous acts on her, and Terri-Lynne hoped to stop it.

For several days, Terri-Lynne testified. She answered question after question relating to Tori's death, and no matter which way they were worded, the answer was always the same. Michael had fantasized about the deed until it became a reality. He had tortured and raped the girl, but it was Terri-Lynne herself who wielded the hammer blows to Tori's tiny skull.

After Terri-Lynne had lured her to Michael's car and then pushed her in, they made their pit stops for drugs and murderous supplies, a claw hammer and garbage bags, and headed out to find the perfect spot for a rape and murder of an eight-year-old baby. Once there, Terri-Lynne took a walk and left Tori and Michael in the front seat. After some period of time, she could hear Michael calling for her, and when she returned, he ordered her to take Tori to urinate. The petite young girl was bleeding, crying and begging Terri-Lynne not to take her back to the car, not to let it happen again. When Terri-Lynne took her back to Michael, this time in the backseat, Tori screamed at her not to leave and tried desperately not to lose hold of her hand. Terri-Lynne broke down herself at that point in the trial, along with most of the jurors and audience. Through her tears she described telling Tori how brave she was as she left her to be violated again and again.

Terri-Lynne walked a short distance away, all the while hearing the screams of one and the grunting laughter of another. She told the court she began to feel as if she were not entirely present in the moment. A flashback situation occurred, and she could feel her own abuses of childhood all over again. The screams and guttural sounds of pleasure spun around in her head like a whirlwind of fall leaves -- different colors but all dark, decaying and absent of love, life and light. She turned, walked with a forceful stride back to the car where Michael's naked legs hung from the back passenger side seat with tiny Tori's body flailing above, and yanked the girl down.

All tools of destruction readily available, she grabbed a garbage bag and claw hammer. Within seconds she had the bag over Tori's head and was pounding the life out of her. Her death could have been caused by any of the kicks and blows

Michael and Terri-Lynne rained upon her small frame. There is no definitive way of knowing how she died. We can only tell it was the result of the severe beating delivered. The only thing known was that Terri-Lynne McClintic and Michael Rafferty were responsible for Tori's death.

On March 16[th,] 2012, Terri-Lynne was asked if she'd like to review the statements she'd made upon arrest before further testimony. It turned out she did. She reviewed and she still agreed with it all. Her only significant objection was that it must be ensured everyone know she committed the murder all on her own. She took the blame. Just as she had promised Michael, she admitted to hearing the screams and feeling the blackout, fuzzy sessions associated with PTSD and admitted to the murder. Again and again she insisted no one was to blame but her for the actual beating death of Tori. She left no question that she was the only participant in the violence that took the life of Victoria.

All throughout March, Terri-Lynne made plans to make a new life and to have new goals in prison. Her plan was to admit guilt and move on. She wanted everything to be over. The whole while, other things were being discovered. On April 1st, jurors visited the murder site. DNA experts testified to the evidence in the car, despite the scrubbing the pair gave it after disposing of Tori's body. A bevy of ex-girlfriends and friends of Rafferty testified as to his behavior and conversations during the time the world was looking for Tori. Michael did not testify in his own defense. Closing arguments for the defense were held on May 7th, 2012. Rafferty's lawyer, Dirk Derstine, desperately tried throughout the trial to paint Terri-Lynne as the mastermind and major player in the murder and gave it one last shot in his closing argument.

Deliberations began on May 10th. Superior Court Judge Thomas Heeney conferred an extended charge to the jury. Nine women and three men retired to consider Rafferty's fate. Canadian law dictates that once the jury is sequestered, publication bans can only be lifted on evidence which the jury did not hear during the trial. That included evidence such as child pornography found on Rafferty's laptop and a four-hour video of Rafferty's cross-examination by the crime squad. The nine women and three men were sequestered with orders to consider the verdicts at approximately 5:40 PM. They re-watched Terri-Lynne's confession video and reviewed other evidence. Deliberations for the evening ended at approximately 8:40 PM after a one-hour break for dinner. At 9:10 they announced the decision that Michael Rafferty was guilty on all three counts he'd been charged with. On May 15th he heard victim impact statements and was sentenced to life without parole chances plus 10 years.

Life After Murder

Terri-Lynne and Michael have begun their lifetime of imprisonment. Michael continues to deny as much guilt as he can, blaming whatever he can on Terri-Lynne. He continues to appeal on the grounds that he should have been considered an accessory after the fact. Terri-Lynne, who had much more jail time under her belt, has settled into her new life. She is still a tough broad and has racked up new charges for attempting to kill a fellow inmate.

If there is any silver lining to this hideously black cloud, it is Tara McDonald. Tori's mother has beaten her addiction and become a doula, helping mothers bring their new souls into the world. She attends health fairs and uses other opportunities to educate new moms as well as those with experience. She has found a way to patch the rips in her soul by encouraging the birth of new lives.

Acknowledgments

Thank you to my editor, proof-readers, and cover artist for your support:

- - Kelly

Aeternum Designs (book cover), Bettye McKee (editor), Dr. Peter Vronsky (editor), RJ Parker Publishing, VP Publications, Lorrie Suzanne Phillippe, Marlene Fabregas, Darlene Horn, Ron Steed, Katherine McCarthy, Robyn MacEachern, Lee Knieper Husemann, Kathi Garcia, Vicky Matson-Carruth, Linda H. Bergeron

Books in the Crimes Canada Collection

An exciting 24-volume series collection, edited by crime historian Dr. Peter Vronsky and true crime author and publisher RJ Parker.

VOLUMES:

(URL LINK ON NEXT PAGE)

1. Robert Pickton: The Pig Farmer Killer by C.L. Swinney
2. Marc Lepine: The Montreal Massacre by RJ Parker

3. Paul Bernardo and Karla Homolka by Peter Vronsky
4. Shirley Turner: Doctor, Stalker, Murderer by Kelly Banaski
5. Canadian Psycho: Luka Magnotta by Cara Lee Carter
6. The Country Boy Killer: Cody Legebokoff by JT Hunter
7. The Killer Handyman by C.L. Swinney
8. Hell's Angels Biker Wars by RJ Parker
9. The Dark Strangler by Michael Newton
10. The Alcohol Murders by Harriet Fox
11. Peter Woodcock: Canada's Youngest Serial Killer by Mark Bourrie
12. Clifford Olson: The Beast of British Columbia by Elizabeth Broderick

View these and future books in this collection at:

rjpp.ca/CC-CRIMES-CANADA-BOOKS

ABOUT THE AUTHOR

Kelly Banaski is a true crime writer and blogger at www.thewomancondemned.com where she writes about her attempts at prison reform and

the interactions it allows with many of America's death row and most infamous women. Her unusual childhood, raised by a career criminal and sometime fugitive, has granted her a unique perspective on inmate issues that manifests itself in many of her inmate relationships. These personal relationships that develop often result in stories that no other writers have access to.

Kelly entered a writing contest for the second annual *Serial Killers True Crime Anthology, 2015, Volume II*, and was selected over several other entries.

Her debut true crime book was *Shirley Turner: Doctor, Stalker, Murderer* (Book 4 in Crimes Canada)

Connect with Kelly

Blog: www.TheWomanCondemned.com

Website: www.KellyBanaski.com

Twitter: @WriteLikeAMutha

Facebook: https://www.Facebook.com/WomanCondemned

Amazon Author Page:

http://amzn.to/1RRtpDX

References

http://www.thespec.com/news-story/2187263-michael-rafferty-the-killer-who-wouldn-t-break/
http://www.thestar.com/news/ontario/2012/02/25/the_main_players_in_the_tori_stafford_murder_case_where_are_they_now.html
https://www.youtube.com/watch?t=149&v=iRevuTlpP1M
http://cnews.canoe.com/CNEWS/Canada/2009/05/22/9534311-sun.html
http://news.nationalpost.com/news/canada/tragedy-struck-after-violent-terri-lynne-mcclintic-met-depraved-michael-rafferty
http://www.canada.com/news/Tori+Stafford+trial+Convicted+killer+describes+luring+Tori/6291529/story.html
http://www.torontosun.com/2012/03/22/mcclintic-was-puppetmaster-defence-lawyer#
http://www.dailyheraldtribune.com/2012/03/06/two-tales-of-toris-last-day-at-school-8
http://www.theglobeandmail.com/news/national/an-innocent-girl-who-was-hunted/article4296500/
http://www.news1130.com/2012/05/15/michael-rafferty-sentenced/
http://www.theglobeandmail.com/news/national/michael-raffertys-evil-defies-explanation/article4184526/
http://www.theglobeandmail.com/news/national/careless-mistakes-were-raffertys-undoing/article4108256/

http://www.dailymail.co.uk/news/article-2114924/Victoria-Tori-Stafford-trial-2012-Final-moments-girl-8-raped-murdered-Woodstock-Ontario.html

https://jl10ll.wordpress.com/tag/murder-of-victoria-stafford/

http://www.obitsforlife.com/obituary/210595/Stafford-Victoria.php

http://www.cbc.ca/news/rafferty-appeal-hitch-1.429646

http://www.theglobeandmail.com/news/national/an-innocent-girl-who-was-hunted/article4296500/?page=2

http://www.thespec.com/news-story/2234853-tara-mcdonald-no-mother-of-the-year-to-tori-stafford/

http://globalnews.ca/news/216561/timeline-victoria-tori-stafford-murder/

https://soundcloud.com/am980/craig-needles-interviews-tara

http://www.lfpress.com/2015/07/30/more-than-six-years-after-her-child-was-slain-tara-mcdonald-is-helping-bring-new-life-to-others

http://news.nationalpost.com/news/canada/tori-stafford-timeline-key-moments-in-the-michael-rafferty-trial

Made in the USA
Monee, IL
22 November 2019